Naked for Tea

Naked *for* Tea

POEMS BY
Rosemerry Wahtola Trommer

ABLE MUSE PRESS

Able Muse Press

www.ablemusepress.com

Printed in the United States of America

Library of Congress Control Number: 2018931565

ISBN 978-1-77349-016-8 (paperback)
ISBN 978-1-77349-017-5 (digital)

Cover image: "Another Sip" by Alexander Pepple
    (with "back story" by Jairo Alzate and "red teacup" by Rafael Bordalo Pinheiro)

Cover & book design by Alexander Pepple

Able Muse Press is an imprint of *Able Muse:* A Review of Poetry, Prose & Art—at www.ablemuse.com

Able Muse Press
467 Saratoga Avenue #602
San Jose, CA 95129

Acknowledgments

I am grateful to the editors of the following journals where many of these poems originally appeared, sometimes in earlier versions:

Beacon: "Inc Lak Keig"

Clover: "What Difference Does It Make"

Dogwood: "We Do It until We Don't"

Encore: "Years Later, I Remember What He Taught Us" and "Poem Not Really about Leaves"

Fungi: "After Many Attempts"

Grand Junction Sentinel: "Come, Wind" and "Fourteenth Way of Looking at a Blackbird"

Gratefulness.org: "One Morning"

Into the Teeth of the Wind: "Not Only with Matches"

Kind of a Hurricane Press: "Dreaming the Apocalypse"

New Verse News: "Picking Up a Hitchhiker in May"

Pinyon: "The Art of Saying Yes"

Poetry of Presence: "Perhaps It Would Eventually Erode, But . . . ," "How It Is," and "A Brief Détente"

Rattle.com: "After My Friend Phyllis Shows Me the *New York Times* Obituary Headline: 'Lou Michaels, All-Purpose Player, Dies at 80, Missed Kicks in '69 Super Bowl'" (winner of "In the News"), "Divining," and "It Won't Make the News" (the preceding two, winners of the "Ekphrastic Challenge")

Reed Magazine: "Dear Erik Satie"

Silver Birch: "With Red Thread"

Sugar Mule: "What Icarus Knew" and "Wild Rose Steps In at the Circus"

Telluride Inside and Out: "Autumnal" and "Going Camping with Audrey Hepburn"

Telluride Watch: "Gretel Explains Herself"

With Infinite Grace

READING ROSEMERRY WAHTOLA TROMMER is to float upon a never-ending waterfall of wonder.

Now. If we are among those fortunate to be so blessed, we will meet our life like this: Open wide in wonder.

Ever-more curious about what may happen next, we will be more willing to be taken by surprise, with each successive moment an unexpected gift to be opened. If we are wise and courageous enough to move at the pace of moments, in each one we will be offered some new gift, some unimagined expression of beauty, courage, grace, fear, loss, exhilaration, peace, anger, love.

Our lives are merely collections of these moments. The way we feel, experience, take in, drink from the fullness of these moments gives shape, over days, weeks, years, to the curving arc of our destiny. They define our intimate, evolving, brief and shining incarnation upon the earth.

Rosemerry Wahtola Trommer cannot help but fall in love with moments.

As you will see, some moments she describes here are simply and exquisitely beautiful. Whole and complete in themselves, with so few lines, holding the entirety of a story in such a small space, as you might hold the tear-moistened face of your child safely in your hands, to make it known, it will all be made right. Some are unavoidably heart-shredding, filled with nearly unspeakable anguish. Still others are almost impossibly ordinary. At times, the moments she describes are *so* ordinary, I remain mystified how Rosemerry can fall so thoroughly and completely in love with even the most ordinary of moments, revealing for us that tiniest invisible sacred thing, so precious, hidden in plain sight. Right there, where we walked past every day year after year never seeing it until the very first time.

Rosemerry's writing gently slows our pace, so she can eventually convince us to stop moving—just long enough to offer a slight nod of her head in that direction, over there, knowing in a moment we, too, will suddenly see something embedded in the world, so unimaginably exquisite—and to which we were blind our entire lives, until that moment: knowing we will always be stopped, to see it, surprised, again, by its very existence. Each time we slow as we pass it by, just for a moment, every day.

Even describing for us the most commonly true thing, the most ridiculously ordinary, she will astonish us awake.

So (it seems fair to ask): How *does* a poem "work" for Rosemerry? How does she know what to say, when does she know precisely how it has to be said,? What does she need to do, or know, or hear in the poem, that lets her know "Ah. . . . There it is?"

I can share two things from my own experience.

First, she will use the language and the form of her poetry to tell the truth. Beyond refusing to exaggerate or use much-too-fancy words, she is so taken by the beauty she finds in each moment—so excited about what she sees, or feels, touches, tastes, or knows—that having described as accurately as she is able how immeasurably perfect that single moment is for her, to add to it would not only be unnecessary; it would take away from the natural holiness already saturating that moment, just as it is.

Second, Rosemerry will fall in love. It seems like every time. With that moment, with that insect, with that melody, with that feeling on her skin, with that image of her son's pants leg too short or too long, even with that pathetic intention of peas steadily climbing the same old string from last year, and the year before. No matter. No matter what the object of her love, if it captures her heart's attention, she will fall in love with it. This is how she comes to know the essence of things, secrets unavailable to so many others striving so desperately to crack the shell of truth in so many things beautiful or true.

For Rosemerry, it seems, all living things will naturally melt open of themselves, if they feel rightly and honorably seen, and known, and truly loved.

Thus every poem, over time, becomes a kind of Rosemerry love poem.

She is not writing "classic" love poems, no Shakespearian sonnets, no Dante adoring the beloved Beatrice from afar, putting the object of their love on a giant pedestal, writing celestial verses of praise about someone with whom they will likely never interact. While the style of the old "masters" might first push away the object of their affection, to such a great distance sufficient to allow them to wax passionate and lyrical (standing somewhere safely far, far away) and go on and on about the eternal nature, the unfathomable eternal depths of their devotion, knowing such love would never be tested by the friction of real human proximity.

Rosemerry instead names those far more difficult, challenging, demeaning, fiercely honest, sloppy, human, incarnate loves we all know well, however often, however terribly we fail at it, again and again.

In this she is fearless. Time and again I find I am bowing to her courage. She grants us audience with Rosemerry, the Woman, in her full stature. Here, we are privileged to walk beside her as she unflinchingly finds her stride: as Poet, Woman, Mother, Wife, Citizen, Daughter of the Family of the Earth.

How can she confess the most painful, the most shameful, the most horrific truths—and with such unquestionable bravery? Her greatest practice, her most effective weapon, the sharpest blade in her arsenal is reserved for her Sword of Love. With it she cuts through the too-easily-seen difficult confusing places in the world. In Love, she patently awaits the slowly emerging, quieter, still, small voices of Truth to reveal their exquisite, sacred, healing manifestation of Beauty, universally invisible to others. Through the eyes of Love, almost anything can become as beautiful as it is.

No matter the object of her love—whether her beloved, or the too-soon brown leaves of an untended plant, the feel of the earth beneath her feet, a taste of honey, a kiss, Beethoven's "Ode to Joy," a cauliflower. There is no hierarchy, each becomes her beloved. Everything we cherish, whether cauliflower, honey, hope, peach, friendship, breathing, is at its center a living thing. Her love of nearly every living thing creates a sanctuary of refuge and safety, and living things then spill their secrets out to her, unbounded pillow talk shared in secret between lovers. Then, she offers us these gems, shares these sumptuous secrets with us, as we become her confidante, her intimate collaborator in these affairs of great love.

Then, at the end of the day, we look back. And we cannot help but see all along the way, so enthralled, so surprised—without ever having named the path she chose for us, never noting the choices we made to go this way, or then that way—throughout this delicious communion of movement and sound, melody and words, we suddenly realize that Rosemerry has subtly and effortlessly revealed to us, with infinite Grace, all the most beautiful, true, essential secrets of life, of Love: of all the whole world.

Pay attention. The elegance of her simplicity will blind you to her mastery. Then, she will let you fall, head over heels, in Love. With everything.

So.

You have been warned.

Wayne Muller

Santa Fe, NM
January 2018

Contents

Feeding Some Deeper Hunger

Another Invisible Road

Lost in the Desert

Naked for Tea

Feeding Some Deeper Hunger

After the Bear Incident

Goldilocks never ate porridge again,
nor did she sit in wooden chairs,
but she spent the rest of her life
looking for another bed
that was just right—
damn perfection, the way
it always makes the rest of the world
so hard, so cold, so not enough.

Though It Is Tough to Choose It

This is the path of failure. We see that our definition of success is what is not working. What is working is deep, unseen.

—Joi Sharp

Even a small discontent is enough to shut us down,
convince us that the world is cold and indifferent.
Everywhere there's evidence of this: The slush

that falls on your car seat when you open the car door.
The carrion eaters with their great black wings
that linger beside the road. You pray for sun,

and it gets darker. Someone asks
you a question, and you see your whole life
fold into one small envelope of failure.

Then one day you hit against the same
impassable wall you always hit, and this time you fall
to your knees, not because you are weak,

but because at last you are ready to be opened.
Oh sweet failure, how it leads us.
Any unhappy ending is only an invitation

to crawl into the blank pages
of the next unwritten chapter.
It was never success that transformed us—

always the breaking. Not the breaking itself,
but the mystery inside pushing through us
like bindweed through pavement,

making cracks in everything
we think we know so that the world
can come streaming in.

Cruciferous

Tonight I have fallen in love with cauliflower,
the way it gives itself so completely
to the soup, the way it informs the curry
with nutty sweetness, with bitterness.
I love the way it turns to cream, how it
loses all sense of its former shape
and is still so wholly present.

I know it is foolish, perhaps, to toss around
a word so important as love, to spend it
on a vegetable. No, I tell myself,
it is worse not to fall in love with cauliflower,
worse to pretend that it isn't a gift,
an invitation to praise. Such simple worship,
a bowl, a spoon, a willing tongue.

The Fourteenth Way of Looking at a Blackbird

Funny how much more beautiful it was
when I thought it was a hawk riding the air,
that crow.

That's Right

I've shown up naked
to tea. I know it's not
the proper thing to do.
In fact, I am a bit surprised
myself to be wearing
nothing more than this pink scarf.
I was wearing more
when I left the house.
At least it is soft, the scarf,
and at least it is warm,
the tea. You don't have
to pretend you don't notice
and I'll not pretend
either. No, let's go on.
That's right,
it's a bit uncomfortable
I suppose, as all things are
at first. We'll go on.
Maybe, by the time we pass the cream
you'll have slipped out of
your own button-up shirt,
your judgment, your embarrassment,
your belt.
Maybe by the time
we get to the bottom
of our cups we'll wonder
why we would ever spend
an afternoon together
any other way.

The Art of Saying Yes

Dear James Joyce, I will come out and say it,
I have forgotten you. Not your name, of course,
and not my general impression of your greatness.
In fact, more than anything I recall you are great,
how I celebrated you, wrote papers praising your genius.

But I do not recall why. I remember more of Andy McTaggert's
second-grade doggerel than I do of you.
In fact, I can still sing all three verses of Andy's song
about Herman the Heron, some silly ditty he made up
and taught me on the merry-go-round. And all I recall

of the hundreds of brilliant pages of your masterpiece *Ulysses*
is "yes, yes, yes, I say yes, yes,"
and that Guinness is good as mother's milk.
It would be embarrassing, James, if I were inclined
to be embarrassed. But no. I am accustomed to losing things,

even things that have been essential to me.
Words I thought I would never forget,
I have lost. Men I thought I would always love,
I have gone for months, even years, without even once thinking
their names. James. You were my everything for a time,

and now, I see your name and think oh, yes, I knew
you once, could name your characters and all your techniques.
I knew where you were born and when and who you married
and what your dad telegraphed when your mother fell ill.
And then the phone rings or I look out the window,

and I am here at the late end of autumn, saying yes
to whoever it is on the other end of the line, saying yes
to the field all golden and high, saying yes to the one
shining crow that without moving its wings
flies from one bare tree to another.

Growing Orbits

Dead end. That is what the sign said.
Funny how long I've believed I could walk only on the road.

It was the deer who showed me how to leap the fence,
how to circle the sign in irregular orbits.

There was no end, then, to the number of paths I might choose.
I was clumsy at first, unversed in this new navigation—

the earth so soft I easily lost my balance.
It was the breath that taught me to pour my weight

first into one foot, then into the other.
My soles relearned how to meet the ground.

It was the clouds that showed me how to let myself
be orchestrated by wind, spiraling like a bird,

as if stirred by some great hand.
Ever since I began circling,

I've come to see dead ends
as invitations.

Given a Window

It's a dangerous thing, the window,
with its curtains pulled to the sides—

it allows you to see through the walls,
but it doesn't allow you to leave.

It shows you another possible world
while you are still shadowed inside.

And what is the voice that says, Jump?
And what is the voice that says, Hide?

And which voice is louder today?
And which voice chants low, a resonant drum?

Jump, it says, Jump, jump, jump,
to hell with the fall, and when you land,

if you're not broken, run.

After My Friend Phyllis Shows Me the *New York Times* Obituary Headline: "Lou Michaels, All-Purpose Player, Dies at 80, Missed Kicks in '69 Super Bowl"

When I die, let them write about
all the mistakes I've made.
Let them mention in the headlines
how many rejection letters
I've received from the *Sun*.
Let them say, "Missed her calling
for Broadway back in 1987."
Let them say, "She trained hard, but
never won a Nordic skate race."
They can note how my children
fought in front of company.
How every chocolate cake
I made sank in the center. How the beets
in my garden were never bigger
than golf balls. How I never even watched
the Super Bowl, much less
knew who played for the Colts
back in 1969 while I was still
forming in my mother's womb
and Lou Michaels missed two
field goals that helped the Jets win.
What do any of us really accomplish?
My friend Wayne says,
"We do what we can

and have mercy." Yes, let
them say I did what I could.
Let them say that I loved
the best I knew how and messed
that up, too. It's what we do,
we who are kicking our way
to the back pages of the paper.
Well intentioned and foundering,
faithful and confused as we are,
we mess up. Yes, mercy on us,
mercy on all our failing little hearts,
how they beat so sincerely, mercy
on this longing to shine, to be brilliant,
this reminder again to kneel.

Wild Rose Steps In at the Circus

And why shouldn't she fill in on the trapeze?
After all, she's no stranger to ropes and heights.
And the Great Flying Sabrina couldn't be all that great.
She'd broken her neck in her last performance,
and that poor little ringmaster looked so cute
in his top hat and tears. Wild Rose struts into
the trailers behind the tent and finds herself a headdress
with red feathers and a red sequin leotard. Really,
how hard could it be? Climb the ladder, grab the bar,
smile and swing, gain momentum, flip three times,
hang from her ankles and spin. Sounds easier
than other things she's supposed to do tonight.
Like make that call to apologize. Never mind what for.
She has other things to think about now, the audience cheering
as she walks into the center ring and lets her robe fall to the floor.

With Red Thread

It was Sam who,
that summer before fourth grade,
danced with me
at the church camp dance
and asked me to walk
outside with him.
"It's hot," he said.
"Let's go look at the stars."
And I, who did not yet
understand the sweet cramping
that tendrilled deep in my gut when
Sam held my hand, said yes.
We stood there a long time,
me looking out at the stars
because that is what
we were there to do.
The night was the color
of Wisconsin violets, crushed,
and Sam, still holding
my hand murmured low, "Oh,
look over there,"
and, when I turned
my feathered head, he leaned
in quick and close
and kissed my astonished lips.
Even thirty-five years later,
I am still somewhat

unprepared as I write
what happened next,
how he sprinted away,
a gleesome hart,
how I stood there, still,
my lips apart, the soft
hands of the night
still holding the most tender
parts of me as they spilled
like fruit no one knew
was yet ripe, and the sharp
stitch of longing so new to me
sewed itself
into my breath
and never left.

Uprising

Speak to me soft
in a voice so low I lean in,

and speak to me in night.
Let's lose any words

that scratch. Let's forget
any tongues that speak in

blades or claws. Speak awe.
Speak pine. Speak blush. Translate

my fear into tenderness.
Converse in amber.

Converse in ice melt clear.
Speak nectar. Speak near

in tones that I more feel
than hear. Speak broken.

Speak wing. Let's mislay our will
to judge. Let us open in honest bloom,

though we're vulnerable to frost.
Let us be fluent in honey,

in greening, in silk. And let
us be freer than that.

Speak in nothing. In the morning,
let's give everything away.

Inner Mary and Martha

All that sweeping and dusting
and straightening I did, O foolish woman,
trying to impress with my efficiency
when what your heart really wanted
was something wild, overflowing with honey
and spilling sweetness all over
those clean, clean floors.

Going Camping with Audrey Hepburn

It is not fancy, the campground,
with the bathroom down the road.
Gravel covers the tent site,
and the number 13 hangs akimbo off
the fence that was once painted brown.
I'm embarrassed to bring Audrey here,
but she sits at the red picnic table
in her simple black dress and diamond tiara
and sips her tea, looking at me over the cup
with her enormous doe eyes and she says
in a voice equal parts romantic and matter of fact:
"Everyone wants to be loved, don't we?
Everyone looks for a way of finding love.
It's a constant search for affection
in every walk of life."

The box elder beetles are not as bad
this year as they were two years ago.
Still, they seem to be everywhere
and one climbs across the table
toward Audrey's tea. She laughs
and brushes its red body away. I want to tell her
yes, yes I want to be loved. And
I have done terrible things in the name
of love, never wanting to hurt anyone.
But I am too nervous to treat her
like a friend. I have her on a pedestal,

though I am beginning to sense
that it is getting in the way. She senses it, too.
"I never think of myself as an icon,"
she says. "What is in other people's minds
is not in my mind. I just do my thing."

A lowrider goes by on the dirt road
beside us, and Eminem smacks the air
with more talk about his mother.
I don't know why it makes both of us laugh,
but we do, perhaps just because it is fun
to laugh. A mosquito lands in the middle
of her forehead, and I hesitate before
giving Audrey a slap, but I do.
And knock over her tea. What is there
to do but offer to make her another cup.
She says yes, and slaps me back.

"When you have nobody you can make
a cup of tea for, when nobody needs you,
that's when I think life is over," she says.
God, she is beautiful, I think, looking
straight into her eyes. That's how I notice
the pedestal is lower, now. Before
I could not see how clear they were,
star-piercing, twin doors long since opened
by a knocking from the inside.

Perhaps It Would Eventually Erode, But . . .

That rock that we
have been pushing up
the hill—that one

that keeps rolling back down
and we keep pushing
back up—what if

we stopped? We are not
Sisyphus. This rock
is not a punishment.

It's something we've chosen
to push. Who knows why.
I look at all the names

we once carved into
its sedimentary sides.
How important

I thought they were,
those names. How
I've clung to labels,

who's right, who's wrong,
how I've cared about
who's pushed harder

and who's been slack.
Now all I want
is to let the rock

roll back to where it belongs,
which is wherever it lands,
and you and I could,

imagine!, walk unencumbered,
all the way to the top and
walk and walk and never stop

except to discover what
our hands might do
if for once they were no longer

pushing.

Trusting Ludwig

It is slow and soft, the first movement—
the right hand sweeping in smooth triple meter,

the left hand singing against it.
Minor, the key, and mysterious

the melody, slow, it is slow and soft,
a walk through moonlight.

What is it that sometimes rises in us,
this urge toward crescendo, toward swell?

I feel it in my hands as they move
across the stoic keys, an urgency,

a reaching toward climax, a pressing
insistence, as if to sing louder is to sing

more true. But over and over again,
Beethoven reminds us, *piano, piano,*

his markings all through the music.
Oh, beauty in restraint. It is soft,

the moonlight, a delicate fragrance,
it is heart opening, the tune,

it is growing in me, this lesson in just
how profoundly the quiet

can move us. And the hands,
as they learn to trust in softness,

how beautifully they bloom.

Divining

written for an unnamed painting by Meghan Tutolo

Not just on the wall—
the writing's on the sky,
the river, the bridge, your hands.

Wouldn't you love to believe
all those blue and red lines
make a map, and if only

you knew how to read those lines,
you might know where to go
from here? Yes, we're all lost

and wrinkling, yes, and surely
doomed, but God, in this moment
between concerns, look, isn't it beautiful,

this place where we wander,
this hour when gold gathers
just before the plum of night?

Once Upon

There is a night you must travel,
alone, of course, though perhaps
there is someone asleep next to you.

The darkness knows exactly what
to say to snap every sapling of hope
that has dared to grow. It poisons

the gardens, even kills the prettier weeds.
For me, it hisses, though perhaps
you have heard a different voice.

The effect is always the same—
a self-doubt that grows up like thorns
around a fabled castle. What

you wouldn't give for sleep.
But it is the awakeness that saves you—
the way that the doubt works

like an unforgiving mirror
and shows you all the places
that most need your attention.

It was never the fairies who bestowed the gifts,
it was doubt all along that entered
you and blessed you so that when

at last the morning came, you were
ready to rise and meet the world, ready
to be your own true love, flawed

though you are, ready to commit
more deeply to serving a story
greater than your own.

Latin 101

As a matter of course, we begin
with the impossible—conjugating love.
Amo, amas, amat.

My son and I sit on the couch and chant
the old syllables that have informed so many tongues.
Amamus, amatis, amant.

It's almost always the first lesson
when learning this language
that few speak anymore.

Every other language I've studied begins
with *to have, to go, to be*, but here we begin
where humans prove our humanness.

I love. You love. He loves.
The news everyday is full of the ways
we fall short. Still, we devote our lives

to these six possibilities.
We love. You love. They love.
Everything depends on this.

Amo, amas, amat.
To my son, they are still only sounds.
He thrills that he can remember them.

But his mother, she wanders the conjugations
like paths, *semitae,* as if stepping through fields
of flowers or war with no idea where the feet

might land next, hoping that though the language
has died, there are still clues in it for the living.
Like where to begin.

Amamus, amatis, amant.
Some lessons are simple to memorize.
Some we practice for a lifetime.

Dreaming the Apocalypse

Sometimes we don't remember to panic.
Sometimes, we just do what needs to be done.
We label. We organize. We make sure that everyone is fed.

It's always more simple than we make it.
All these questions. Just find the food.
Feed the people. Stop feeling guilty.

We know no one will understand.

*

There is a floor beneath the floor.
What we think is the foundation
is only another surface.

What really holds us up is uneven,
unknowable, transformative. It is always
changing. It cannot be labeled.

What you cannot see changes you.

*

This isn't all. What it means to hold things—
this changes, too. Once we thought
we were the ones who did the holding.

Now we see that we are being held.
Once we thought we were hiding.
Now we see that there is no one

to tell the truth to except to ourselves.

*

There is so much that we
can never explain. Already
I know I have lost you.

I'm sorry, but I am not sorry.
It has nothing to do with what you've done.
Isn't it almost funny, well, maybe not yet,

how we once thought change was a problem?

Quantum

on a line from Ocean Vuong

The most beautiful part of your body
is the place your lover has just kissed,

how his lips remind you that you are also
orchid and apple and arch.

How easy it is to forget our own holiness.
How sweet when another reminds us of the ocean

still in our blood, the sand in our hair.
Call it communion, the way he touches you

and the way your own tongue leaves
a wet trail on his skin not so different

from those first attempts to crawl onto shore.
The most beautiful part of your body

is your longing to open more, everywhere
he touches, you become door.

Another Invisible Road

Cut Deep

Picking up broken glass
with bare hands,
of course I was cut,
but something in me
was curious to learn
the secrets of being sharp.
Something in me
was grateful
for another reason
to be tender
with everyone I meet.

Poem Not Really about Leaves

I forgot them, the impatiens
that I had left out on the deck. I forgot
them on the coldest night of the spring.
Sure they looked okay in the morning,
but by afternoon, they were darkened
and sullen and droopy things, dead.
How many times have I neglected
the ones that I love? How many
nights have I left them in the cold,
not for lack of love, but out of simple
absentmindedness? It is not that I didn't
expect the cold, but I was distracted
with my own small sufferings.
Sometimes I'm sorry is not enough.
That is when I promise myself
to do better, to be more aware,
more generous, less blinded
to what's happening all around me
in the world. But soon enough,
there's this wound and this deadline,
this loss and this wish, and I just
don't notice how cold it is,
the thermometer dropping,
the quiet leaves doing what leaves do.

Gretel Explains Herself

All those crumbs I left
on the path, it's not
that I want to go back,

it's just that I happen to like
wild birdsong wherever I go.

United

For three and a half hours,
the man in 25 D and I
sit beside each other
and do not speak.

Somewhere, I like to imagine,
is a woman who wishes
that it were she
who got to be the woman

sitting in 25 E. I wonder
what she is doing right now,
perhaps twirling a strand
of her hair and remembering

the way his voice warms
when he says her name.
It occurs to me
that in every seat is a human

who loves and who wants
to be loved. A plane
of lovers, we are,
all of us politely minding

our elbows, traveling
with our seat belts low
and tight across our laps.
And though we've never

met before and will likely
never meet again, and though
we may not even speak
to each other as we fly,

just think of it,
all that love moving
across the country
in a dark and turbulent sky.

The Practice

Remember, says my friend, to look
for beauty every day. And immediately

I think of the blue heron I saw this afternoon
as it flew upriver, its elegant neck tucked

into its body in flight, its deep, slow wingbeats
guiding it through the curves of the wide canyon.

In my chest, I felt it, the rising urge to fly,
the pulsing, the thrill of blue heron.

In that instant, I did not wonder
if a moment of beauty is enough

to sustain us through difficult times.
I knew only that I had to remind my eyes

to watch the highway instead of following
the great blue weight as it wove

through the empty cottonwood tops,
its silhouette charged with improbable grace,

its long legs dangling behind,
a reminder we all must land sometime.

One Definition of Faith

toeing the edge
of everything
we think we know—
spreading a picnic blanket for us
on the other side

We Do It until We Don't

Sometimes it seems as if everyone
in the world is lonely, all of us
shuffling around, slumped by the weight

of our singular lonelinesses. As if
we all drank the same sad tea.
As if our loneliness also makes

us blind and deaf to each other,
unable to see that everyone else
is as broken and blemished as we are.

Every time we think we find
an answer, some path to wholeness,
it turns out to be another dead end.

How could we all be so lost together?
Sometimes there is a light inside
the loneliness. And it grows

and it grows more and more intense,
as if to say, "There is so much light."
But that is not the answer we were

looking for, and so we go on searching,
carrying our loneliness like a basket
full of dark black stones,

somehow not noticing
that we could put it down
any moment, even now.

Come, Wind

I am starving for winter.
There is too much bloom in me.
Tuck me into the season of emptiness
and shadow and deep, unfathomable snow.
Teach me to be unrecognizably myself,
the everything that isn't, the generous
space between. Let there be no one here
who knows how to answer. Let the wind reshape
anything it finds.

Wild Rose Goes for a Drive with God

But first, she takes a few slugs of absinthe.
The pale green thrill of it blazes in her throat.

God walks in just as she finishes her glass.
God finishes the bottle. Then he says,

Are you nervous? Wild Rose doesn't hesitate
to say, No way. I am ready for anything.

God says they're going for a spin.
Wild Rose doesn't care where. All she wants

is for God to show her a real good time. And
she is open to what that means. Here,

says God, as they arrive at the car,
climb in. He opens the driver's seat door for her.

She pours her long legs in. There's no brake, she sees.
No rearview mirror. No reverse. No safety belts.

A big back seat. Oh yeah, she says, and revs the engine.
The night smells like licorice, like sweat.

Joyful, Joyful

From the back row, no one can see
that the flute player's white oxford shirt
is misbuttoned. His dirty blonde hair
falls into his eyes. He tosses it back
with a flick of his head, picks up his instrument
and focuses his attention on the conductor.

With a lurch, the sixth-grade band launches
into the last section of Beethoven's Ninth,
and the familiar tune of "Ode to Joy"
brightens the dim auditorium.

The conductor keeps perfect time,
and the students, though stilted,
follow her rhythm. I think of Vienna,
1824, in the Theater am Kärntnertor,
when Beethoven himself stood on stage
at the end of his career to direct the premiere,
his first time on stage in twelve years.

Though he could not hear the symphony, he furiously
waved his arms in tempo, moving his body
as if to play all the instruments at once,
as if he could be every voice in the chorus.

And when it was done, the great composer
went on, still conducting, not knowing
it was over until the contralto soloist moved to him
and turned him to face the ovation.

With the greatest respect, and knowing
that applause could not reach him,
the audience members raised their hands and hats
and threw white handkerchiefs into the air,
then rose five times to their feet.

When the sixth-grade band director
lowers her arms, the young musicians stop with her.
They rise and bow, and the audience claps
and some of the parents whoop.
And the students bow again, and again,
though the clapping is done.
They do not yet know how to carry pride
in their awkward bodies, and they stumble
and list off the stage.

The flute player's black pants are too short
for his long thin legs. He is growing in ways
neither he nor his mother can understand.
There she is, weeping in the back row,
in her ears, in her heart, a song
no one else can hear.

Gift

Here, she said, her pockets
stuffed with forgiveness,
borrow some of mine.
I take it between my fingers
like a coin and hold it up
to see how it shines,
but I hide it quick,
almost embarrassed
to be seen with it.
All day, I touch my pocket
to be sure it's still there.
All day, I dream of ways
to spend it.

How It Might Continue

Wherever we go, the chance for joy,
whole orchards of amazement—

one more reason to always travel
with our pockets full of exclamation marks,

so we might scatter them for others
like apple seeds.

Some will dry out, some will blow away,
but some will take root

and grow exuberant groves
filled with long thin fruits

that resemble one hand clapping—
so much enthusiasm as they flutter back and forth

that although nothing's heard
and though nothing's really changed,

people everywhere for years to come
will swear that the world

is ripe with applause, will fill
their own pockets with new seeds to scatter.

Another Invisible Road

See, he says,
his hand an invitation,
see how to this side
the trees are slender
and on this side
how large they are.
We can imagine,
he says, that a post road
went through here
and on one side of it
the forest was cleared.
On the other side is old growth.
I look, and agree, though
now there is no hint
besides the trees
that this was once
a well-traveled way.
I think of all the people
who have walked
through my life,
how invisible their paths
are now. Can anyone else
see the ways I've been marked?
Some brought invasive seeds.
Some made light.

*

We hear it
long before we see it—
zee zee zee zoo zee.
A trout lily
bows by the stream.
Open, its six yellow petals peel back.
zee zee zee zoo zee.
Do you know why it's bowed?
Paul asks me.
I like that he will know the answer.
Inside, he says, are all the sex organs,
and they do not want to get wet.
zee zee zee zoo zee.
He explains,
one way other flowers
stay dry is to learn to close up
whenever things get dark.
Now that's smart.
But I think to myself,
Learn to bow.

*

What is this drive
toward opening?
Here: white trilliums
and anemone, pink spring beauties
and ten thousand
blue and yellow violets
all unfold in a mass
affirmation of life
longing for itself.
The beech leaves are
so intent on unfurling
that their bud scales are bursting
and fall from the canopy
like coppery rain in our hair.
zee zee zee zoo zee.
Even this damp land
beneath our feet
is still opening—a widening canyon
carved over 340,000,040 years
by water moving toward the sea.
One day, we'll be put
into this earth forever.
For now, there's this
bird to find, there's this
drive toward opening.

*

And there it is,
the black-throated green warbler.
It's yellow. Though I can't tell
from this distance
where its silhouette flits to
high in the trees.
I thrill to see it,
but the bird is not why I am here.
I have no list to check.
I don't know why I am here.
Except that it feels good
to walk in the woods
amongst hemlock and beech
and wild cherry and to hear
the stories about how it is.
How the barberry came
and never left. How the
Henslow's sparrow ushers
in the summers here, *tsi-lick, tsi-lick,*
tsi-lick. How the male toads,
when they're ready to mate,
will grip onto your finger
and not let go. How quietly
someone might walk into your life
and change the landscape,
another invisible road.

Inc Lak Keig

A woman walks down the street.
It does not matter her name,

the color of her hair, her age,
or how she votes. What matters

is if you would go help her rise
if she falls or is weeping.

Yes, what matters is if you look openly
into her eyes when she is seeking tenderness.

What matters is if
you see how she, like you,

is holding onto something dead
and has not quite yet managed

to let it go. There are cultures
where people greet each other,

strangers and lovers, by saying,
I am you, I know this so deeply inside.

What counts is if,
when you see another creature

you sense something of the magnificent
oneness that holds us all.

Vivian Learns to Ride a Bike

After the training wheels come off
she wobbles and crashes and jumps up
to cry again. She pushes her helmet back
into place and rubs her hands of the gravel.
I force myself not to offer advice. Some
things must come from the center.

Vivian picks up the bike and straightens
the wheels, finds her place on the seat.
The pedals are not too far for her to reach.
She is ripe for this skill, and mostly willing.
She jerks on the handlebars, overrights

herself and falls again. There is such a thing
as too much right. She once told me
that if you do not learn to cartwheel
before you are eight, then you never will.
Something in the vestibular system, I wonder.

I don't know if it's true, but I do know
there are certain windows that close.
An eye that is unused in the first few months
of life will never learn to see, though
its parts are all in working order. Perhaps

there are windows for the heart, too,
so that if by a certain age it does not learn how
to get up and try again after it has fallen,
it will stay down and never learn how
to love beyond itself. *Come on,*

I say under my breath, *you can do it,*
Come on, I say to my heart. And then out loud I say,
Yes, yes, dear girl, you are doing it.
You are doing it, I say as she falls,
falls again, and gets back up.

It Won't Make the News

for the painting "Chronicle" by Ruth Bavetta

What we really need is to gather
in the street and talk to each other.
Any street. Lined with shrubs
or tenements. Paved or dirt
or cobblestone. With orange cones
or with wooden barriers
to set off the block so we can talk,
can talk and listen and watch the day go by.
Some will join us. They will wonder
why we've gathered. They'll
pull out their binoculars
as if there's something more to see.
There's always something more to see,
like the way the light comes through the hedge
and makes it more gold than green.
Hey, did you hear that nightingale?
When's the last time you heard one?
All my life I've been too busy. Rushing
from one here to the next. But look
what happens when we gather
in the street and gawk in whatever
direction. We start to become a we—
you, me, the man in the yellow plaid shirt,
the cop, the woman in white tennis shoes.
It does not matter how we vote or

where we've been or how much we make
or if we pray, here we are in the same place
on the same day. Not because someone died,
not because someone's done something wrong.
There is no one to cheer for but us.
We'll go back to our homes soon enough,
but for now, here we are
doing the most important work,
gathering in the street to notice together
the scent of fall, the warmth of mid-afternoon sun,
the way all our shadows fall the same direction.

How It Is

Over and over we break
open, we break and
we break and we open.
For a while, we try to fix
the vessel—as if
to be broken is bad.
As if with glue and tape
and a steady hand we
might bring things to perfect
again. As if they were ever
perfect. As if to be broken is not
also perfect. As if to be open
is not the path toward joy.

The vase that's been shattered
and cracked will never
hold water. Eventually
it will leak. And at some
point, perhaps, we decide
that we're done with picking
our flowers anyway, and no
longer need a place to contain them.
We watch them grow just
as wildflowers do—unfenced,
unmanaged, blossoming only
when they're ready—and my God,
how beautiful they are amidst
the mounting pile of shards.

Not Only with Matches

While lighting the fire
she also lit the curtains,
the sofa, her long brown hair.
It wasn't what she had meant
to do, but there was no water
anywhere and in the end
even if there had been,
she was too busy being consumed
with how the leaping flames were tides,
how the colors changed from red
to redder, to blue, how impossible
it was to be anywhere else,
and how the fire did not inquire nor care
which parts of her were good,
which parts were bad—
it just took everything.

Waiting

You see the late summer clouds
and you know their gray
is the shade of gray
that ends in a mudslide,

and then comes the rain
you knew would come,
stiff rain and merciless.

But this is not about
the wall of mud that eventually
finds every room of your house.
This is about the waiting—

when you are aware
of the years inside each minute,
when you have plenty of time

to put on your boots
and grab your shovel
and your hat and your coat
and stand out in the rain

before there is any sign of mud
creeping down the hills,
that interval while the destruction

is still just an idea,
the inside of your home
still clean, still dry.

Story Problem

If I were paddling in a green canoe
traveling a rate of x miles per hour

and if you were paddling in a blue canoe
traveling at a rate of y miles per hour,

and the rate of the stream is a constant,
which already we know is a lie,

then how hard would we need to paddle,
where force equals g, before the canoes

were not canoes, but a field of rye in which
you and I are wading together

through the grass waist high and golden
and no longer traveling in separate canoes?

And let's say in this field there's a breeze
traveling from the west at p miles per hour,

then if I tossed you a dream
and you were standing due east of me,

how long would it take the dream to reach you?
And what is the percentage of a chance

the dream might come true? Not enough facts,
and too many irrelevant details,

but of course it matters that the field was golden,
though I wouldn't mind if it were green

filled with blue flax flowers all bobbing in the breeze
still traveling from the west at p miles per hour—

yes, a whole river of blue flowers nodding at us
as if to say, that's right, there are no answers

that make any sense. It's okay,
just keep on telling the story.

Without a Doubt

Could be you feel
like a tiny bird.
Even the loveliest nests
become traps,
and so you fly.
You tell yourself
you know where you
are meant to go
and you map and you plan
and fly straight into the wind.
Could be no matter
how hard you flutter
you arrive nowhere,
and that flying
becomes a new kind of trap.
All that fluttering
exhausts you
until wings wearied,
will spent,
certainty lost,
you turn away
from whatever it is
you thought
you must fly toward.
And then perhaps
you understand
that wherever the wind

is going to go
it will go. Could be
you find yourself
saying yes to the wind.
Could be that it
is so beautiful,
this new kind of flying,
that you forget
to be frightened when you don't know
what will happen next.
Could be you've never
been quite so aware
how sweet the invitation
to let yourself be carried,
how unbounded a story, the sky.

Crossing the Line

Mi casa es su casa.
My arms are your arms.

My lips are your lips.
My ripeness, yours. My triceps,

yours. My hunger, my nipples,
my skin, my swollen pinks

are yours, yours. And why stop there?
My dry elbows, your elbows.

My bunions, your bunions.
My cyst, your cyst. What part

of me would you rather not love?
Could you miss it? Tell me you will also take

my thinning skin, my widening hips,
my wrinkled cheek, my cracked heel.

If my fear is your fear; my ugly,
your ugly; my broken, your broken;

my shame, your shame, please,
come to *mi casa, mi casa es su casa,*

my forgiveness your forgiveness,
my laughter yours.

Lost in the Desert

What Difference Does It Make?

So Eve said to the snake,
I don't really like fruit,
and the snake said to Eve
that the story would sound
much better down the line
with an apple instead
of a forbidden parsnip.
No one craves parsnips anyway,
he hissed. No one would believe
in the centuries to come
that a woman would risk everything
for a root. He was the kind
of snake that knew
what a difference
the right symbol can make.
Nope, said Eve, I'm just
not into apples. So
the snake did what any
snake would do, he
offered her what she
wanted, a parsnip,
with cream-colored flesh
and cream-colored skin,
and she bit
as he knew she would do,
but then he lied about it all,
said she'd eaten the apple.

It was better this way,
this lie so small, just one
tiny seed inside a much
greater garden.

At the Border

There it was, tacked up
against my heart,
the No Trespassing sign.

I forgot I had posted it
until today when I found it,
by accident really, while wandering

in a place I've neglected
for a long, long time. Though
it was rust stained and crooked,

the message was clear.
I was surprised to find it here.
Though now it makes more sense

why you have not come closer
as I've wished you would.
It's gone now, darling, the sign

with its capital letters
and Day-Glo warning. Nothing left
but the holes where the nails were.

I know it is easier to notice
when something is added
than it is to notice when something

is taken away. That's why I mention it.
In case you were blinking when I took
it down. In case it is not too late.

Morning Commute

Red carcass beside the road,
the thin ribs like white staffs
and the black birds
that flitter around them
like staccato notes
escaped from the score—

if you listen for a death song
all you'll hear
is the shiny caw of good fortune,
the sound of your own
hungry wheels humming by.

The Precious Matter of Love

Why just ask the donkey in me
to speak to the donkey in you
when I have so many other beautiful animals
and brilliant colored birds inside
all longing to say something
exciting and wonderful to your heart?
    —Hafiz, tr. Daniel Ladinsky, "Why Just Ask the Donkey"

Dear, though I have come to you
as many other beautiful animals—
long-necked swan and Persian cat—

though I have worn for you
my most vermillion feathers and
sung to you with the voice of the bird

that always disappears before it can be named,
though I have come to you as lamb, as heron,
please, do not refuse my donkey.

Too curious and stubborn, all tug and bray,
gray and dull and smelling of dung,
of course you would want to turn away.

But please, if you can, meet me this way,
when I am awkward and stepping
on my own feet, yours, too. Meet me

when I am unlovable and love me then.
Though I stink. Though I am not graceful
nor lovely nor easy, but strong. And here

I am, nuzzling your hand as it opens, aspiring to
be nowhere but here. Dear, we are nothing
but flesh for life to push through. I am done

hiding inside the bright wings, or even,
for that matter, beneath the dun hide.
Only a heart touches another heart.

Here is mine.

Note to Self above the Paradox Valley

You do not need to know what comes next.
There is always another storm, and you
cannot hang the tent out to dry before
it has gotten wet. You cannot shovel snow
that has yet to fall.

Put down the shovel. Breathe
into the dark spaces of your back,
feel how they open like cave doors
to let in the light.
Let your face soften. Let the creases
fall out of your brow. The mind,
no matter how clear, will never become
a crystal ball.

Whatever is wisest in you knows to run
when it hears the first crashes of rock fall.
It does not pause then to consider
metamorphic or igneous,
nor does it hesitate to wonder
what might have pushed them down.
It is no small thing to trust yourself.

It is right that love should shake your body,
that you should find yourself trembling
in the rubble and dust
after all your certainties come down.

But your breath has not left you.
Here is the morning rain. It opens
the scent of the leaves, of the air.
All around you the world is changing.

What are you waiting for?
Here is the cup of mint tea
growing stronger in itself.
Here on this cliff of uncertainty
there is a stillness in you
so spirited, so alive
that whatever is wisest in you
is dancing.

Wild Rose Chooses a Tail

She has had enough of this tight-assed
skinny-hipped nonsense,
walking down the street like a rail,
like a pole, like a wall.
Wild Rose moves in curves.
She is more swank, more sway everyday.
And she wants some tail.
Not some fluffy little scut.
Not a prehensile appendage
always grabbing at things.
She wants a long and slinky
swirl of tail that swings
when she steps, and you can bet
she will swing it for the pure
fun of swinging. She wants to swish
it and flick it with the wiggle in her gait,
'cause she's got fanny
and flair and a swagger in her ramble,
and now, she's got herself a tail . . .
well, you know she's been looking
for another way to tease
anyone who thinks a woman's
is supposed to play it straight,
and that new tail,
it rocks it on her coccyx,
and the way she's feelin',
mmm hmmm, the road
can go on forever.

After Many Attempts

Just because it wasn't here yesterday
doesn't mean it won't be here today.

Some things arrive only in their own time.
Just because I am talking about morels

doesn't mean I'm not talking about love.
And here it is, golden and misshapen,

something I step over once before discovering.
Isn't it wonderful when sometimes

we choose to show up and then, well,
it's not really an accident, is it,

that we find ourselves
with our hands, our hearts so full.

Butterfly Effect

My son comes in, hands cupped
and asks me for a jar. What for?
I ask, and he lets me peek between

his palms to see the butterfly.
The boy is all aglow with the catching of it,
and I do not try to hide my regret.

Let it go, I say, it will be so much happier, love.
No, he shouts, and looks about
for a jar since I won't help him out.

Please, I say, let it go,
but he is intent on keeping
what feels valuable. He pokes holes

in the lid so the admiral can breathe,
gives it a yellow salsify and insists
that it's sipping nectar. The butterfly,

all violent wing, flaps a long time before
settling beside the pretty weed.
The boy stares in the jar at his butterfly.

It is pure, his admiration for the
loveliness he sees, so pure that I squeeze him
tight, too tight perhaps, my arms

around the place he would have wings.

When the Counselor at the Sex for Parents Talk Asked Us What We Wished Someone Had Told Us about Sex When We Were Younger, I Remember

We were ten-year-old girls
huddled around the book
that Stacia's mother had given to her,
and we read in chorus the names of the body parts,
penis, vagina, labia, testicles,
the words tasted like foreign food on our tongues—
so strange they made us giggle—
and there was something else,
a pull in my belly, a breathlessness
inside my voice
as I read out loud for the others
all about how the act was done.
There was nothing in the book
about love or even the violet crush
of lust. Just the facts about
how the bodies fit and the science
of what might happen then
when the sperm fertilized the egg.
The authors did not mention
how diamonds might explode
through your toes, did not mention
gasping or humming or moans—
no, mostly we wondered why
anyone would ever want

to do what they showed
on page 29, that page we
couldn't quite stop
our hands from returning to
so we could stare
at those bodies
so impossibly joined,
again, again.

Lots of Honey

Before she sleeps, my daughter and I
face each other on her pillow,
our heads heavy, our eyes half mast,

and in the dim light we recite
"The Owl and the Pussycat"—
the words seem to leap between

our breaths so that we can't tell
where each other's voice ends or starts,
and I think of the pericardium

around the heart, which the Chinese say
is a boundary place that decides
who gets in and who stays out,

and I marvel at how, for now,
on this quiet night, our hearts
seem to need not any space apart,

and after the owl and the pussycat
dance to the light of the moon, the moon,
we curl into each other's curves

like two parentheses
on the same side of a thought,
like twin silver runcible spoons.

Encounter

It was, perhaps, the Virgin
herself who passed me

on the street today, but
without her halo, without

her donkey, I did not recognize her.
She did not ask for help,

not exactly, but she wore
the look of the lost

and something else—
a manner of dignity.

It was only hours later
I let her into my thoughts.

There's not a lot
of room in there,

so I offered her the stable.
She took it. When my son

points out the stars tonight,
I can't help but think

they look brighter
than usual. Look, I say

to the part of me that would
close the door to her,

would close to anyone,
look, I say, how easily

one person can enter
into even the lowliest

place we offer them and make
the world shine.

Positively

Saying yes to too many things at once
is like eating dark chocolate truffles one
after another after another. The first

is infused with wild raspberry, which leads
to a caramel truffle with *fleur de sel,* which leads
to two smooth champagne truffles, which leads

to a tummy ache, bittersweet. My calendar
has a tummy ache. Its numbered squares
are filled in with rows of rich invitations . . .

a book club infused with Louise Erdrich
and Sauvignon Blanc, a meditation retreat
handcrafted with extra silence, a trail run

through aspen groves filled with silky light.
How could I pass on any of these delights?
Saying yes to too many things at once

is like crossing a remote border at midnight,
and though your pulse races with the thrill,
you have no idea if you will ever know

what home means again. Saying yes
to too many things at once is in fact
a disguise for saying no. No to openness,

no to spontaneity, no to whatever surprise
might have found its way into the vacant
possibility of that deliciously empty square.

Gas Station Eucharist

Not at all like the body and blood
of Christ, this Diet Pepsi and bag
of Barbara's Jalapeño Cheese Puffs,
but I take it in, feeling blessed
despite the fact that I have seen
what cola will do to an engine.
Perhaps that is what I am hoping
for—the kind of god that will
scour me at the same time
I lick my fingers and hunger
for more.

A Brief Détente

From across the pond,
the doe and I regard each other—
she with enormous brown eyes,

I with my hands full of empty.
We take turns pretending
we're not watching each other,

but we are, aware
of each other's slightest move.
She goes back to her eating.

I go back to shaking
the dried iris pods
to see if they rattle. They do.

She startles
but does not run to the trees.
I am oddly relieved

as she interests herself again
in the grass spiking out of the snow.
All day a feeling of doom

has settled in me, a heavy,
unshakable dark. It doesn't lessen
because of the doe, but perhaps

it does. She lifts her head again
for something I do not hear or see,
and I, too, tense, before we return

to the fragile moment, this small act
of trusting each other, witnesses
to the cold in the air,

the ice already cured on the pond,
the day losing
whatever color it had left,

the iris seeds spilling
their dark, latent praise
atop the snow.

Picking Up a Hitchhiker in May

The burial of the dead is Humanity 101.
  —Thomas Lynch, undertaker and poet, NPR Interview

It's messy when they die
in winter, he says. The dirt
is too cold to work with then.
I tell him I will consider this
when I die. Just give me two weeks'
notice, he says, quoting a joke,
and it occurs to me humor
must be an unwritten
prerequisite for a gravedigger.
I ask him what he thinks
about the recent uproar in Boston,
no one wanting the bomber
buried in their own backyard.
Well, he says, I've always thought
we should have a special section
for the politicians. We could put
him here with them—in a place where
we let the dogs run.
In the space before I laugh,
I remember the story
the undertaker told about how
in the middle ages they considered
suicide the ultimate crime.
But since you can't punish a dead man,

they took out their ire on his corpse
and buried it at a crossroads
to be trod on forever. He said,
"If we do not take care of dead humans,
we become less human ourselves."
The man next to me says,
"You know, I give every person I bury
the gravedigger's promise."
We are almost to the cemetery gate.
"I say, I'm the last person who's ever gonna
let you down, and the last one
who'll ever throw dirt on you."
He laughs a laugh so real
I can smell the earth thawing in it.

What Icarus Knew

Of course I know
what happens to wax
when a woman flies
too close to the sun.
It has been done,
been done before
and it will be done
again, because
the first thing to melt
is the will to stop
flying toward
the most beautiful thing
you ever felt.

Dear Erik Satie,

Thank you for the *Gnossienne No. 2,* and for the directions you wrote above the staves. "With amazement," you wrote, at the start of the piece. That is what I told my hands as they bumbled tonight through the melody. Thank you for the melody. Just today I saw with amazement the four plover eggs still intact in the nest by the river's edge, though I could tell by the wet silt around them that midsummer's high water had covered them. My friend said she thought they might not hatch. I watched as the mother plover ran along the shore, pretending she had a broken wing, attempting to distract us. "I think they will hatch," I said, though the words were said more out of longing than belief.

Sometimes longing is all we have. "Don't leave," you wrote in the score. That's what I thought later today when I saw the lonesome duckling in the pond—no mother, no father, no other baby ducks. I longed to be a mother duck, to know what a baby duck might need. As it is, I gave it space, knowing sometimes giving space is the most generous thing we can do. I do not want space. Tonight I saw a picture of my friend with her newborn girl, both of them naked, skin to skin. That is what I want. "With great kindness," you say, and that is the way I want to live this song of life—in amazement and with great kindness—to know myself as the kind of melody that might be played poorly and still sound beautiful because the hands that played me did it "lightly, with intimacy," though the keys keep changing, though the timing is unmarked, though the song doesn't end anywhere near where it begins.

As the Broken Do

May I be wrong. May I come
to you without my books,
without my rules, without
my shoulds. Let me always
arrive at your door with empty hands.

Let me meet you with my pockets
full of blank, not convinced
of anything except
the possibility of everything.

Let me be wrong. Let me not label anyone
a liar. Let me bottom out.

What is it in us that wants to be right?
I have seen it turn a whole month, a whole life
to ice. I have felt the chains of certainty,
I have worn the shackles of listen-to-me.

Let me be wrong. Let there be chinks
in my belief. Let there be splinters
in my conviction. Look how alone it is
in this hour when I am so perfectly right.

May my rules go begging. May my imperatives
learn to crawl. May my righteousness hold
an empty bowl. May my musts all redden to rust.
And may I be wrong as the wrongers are wrong.
And may I unknow. And unlearn.
And unselve. And love as the lovers love.

The Tiger Comes to Visit the Hunter

Yes, they're big claws.
I have not come to hurt you.
Though I could. And yes,
these teeth devour flesh.
You are lovely flesh, but
I am not here to eat.
I have come to your cave
so we both might sleep.
Perhaps it is a test.
See how I let you keep your blade.
See how I curl on the floor,
my neck exposed, how I close my eyes.
No one will die tonight.

What She Really Wants

When she is drought,
be rain, and when
she is rain, be cup.
When she is lost,
let her be her own map,
and when she is wind
be wind. There are trees
in her, whole orchards.
Be soil and sunshine and bee.
When she is seed,
be time. When she
is moon, be sea.

One Morning

One morning we will wake up and forget
to build those barriers we've been building,
the one between us that causes tears,
the one we've been creating
for years, perhaps out of some sense
of righteousness and boundary,
perhaps out of habit.

One day we will wake up
and let our empty hands
hang empty at our sides.
Perhaps they will rise,
as empty things sometimes do
when blown by the wind.
Perhaps they simply will not remember
how to frighten, how to grasp.

We will wake up that morning
and we will have misplaced all our theories
about why and how and who did what
to whom; we will have mislaid
all our timelines of when and plans of what
and we will not scramble
to write new strategies we know will not satisfy us.

On that morning, not much else
will have changed. Whatever is blooming
will still be in bloom.
Whatever is wilting
will wilt. There will be fields
to plow and trains to load and children
to feed and work to do.
And in every moment,
in every action, we will
feel the urge to say thank you,
we will follow the urge to bow.

Autumnal

after a line from William Stafford

When the leaves are about to yellow and fall
ask me then how I tried to hold on to what was green,
how I thought perhaps I was different,
how everything I thought I knew about gold
turned brittle and brown. Ask me what it was like
to fall then. Sometimes the world's workings feel transparent
and we know ourselves as the world. Sometimes
the only words that can find our lips are thank you,
though the gifts look nothing like anything
we ever thought we wanted. Sometimes, gratitude
arrives in us, not because we are willing,
but because it insists on itself, like a weed,
like a wind, like change.

Years Later, I Remember What He Taught Us

The guide stabbed the small round of cactus with his knife,
then held it up in front of him. With his other hand,
he flicked on his lighter and burned off the spines.
I do not remember the smell of it, nor how much it smoked.
What I remember is how he was left with a smooth and harmless
lump of green in his palm. He sliced it open and taught us to drink.
It could save you, he said, if you find yourself lost in the desert.

Do this. Burn off your spines. Whatever bristles you have grown
to protect yourself, set them aflame. Open however you can,
let me pull you to my lips. I will do the same for you.
We are all lost in the desert.

How It Feels

Remember that day
when you felt as if
there were two sumo wrestlers
inside your gut? Remember
how they whumped and slammed
each other and your whole body
felt bruised with their weight?

That was the day you promised
yourself you would never
compromise your integrity
ever, ever again. But
here you are, considering
how to cut off your limbs
to fit into someone else's box.

It's no mistake you are back here,
a wrestling ring in your gut.
There is more to learn
and unlearn about who you are
and who you are becoming.
And those big ol' sumo wrestlers?
They'll get tired, and when they do,
offer them tea in very small cups.
Ask them where they've been so long.
And when they finish their sipping,
cheer them on as they start to fight again,
making in you more space
than you've ever felt inside before.

How It Goes On

On the day I learned that he died,
I made blackberry jam. The kitchen
was steamy and hot from the water bath,
and the bubbling saucepan of fruit took nearly
an hour to gel. I stood and stirred
and stirred and stood. The sweet scent
touched everything. It was gray
outside and smelled of rain, while in
the pot deepened a most beautiful darkness,
the color of sugar that comes with time.
It was an accident, of course, the kind
that makes every one of us think
we are lucky to be alive, lucky to stand
wherever we are standing, whether
it's in line for a bus or beside the road
or in front of a chalkboard or
in the middle of the kitchen stirring
blackberry jam. How could I not fall in love
with the heat, with the color of blackberries?
How could I not fall in love with the cat
and the chatter of the girl playing dolls
and the racket of the boys throwing pillows
and even the ache in my feet? What a blessing
to be alive, to feel this awful tug
in my gut, this surge of what if,
this swell of what was, this terrible gift
of standing for hours to preserve what is sweet

as if I believe there will be a day months from now
when we will eat the sweetness and
know ourselves lucky to be alive.

p. 6: "Though It Is Tough to Choose It" epigraph is from my notes from a private conversation: I've been studying with Joi Sharp, a Satsang teacher, since 2005. To learn more about Joi and her work, visit www. joisharp.com.

p. 9: "The Fourteenth Way of Looking at a Blackbird" is written in conversation with "Thirteen Ways of Looking at a Blackbird" by Wallace Stevens, from *The Collected Poems of Wallace Stevens* (Vintage, reprint edition, 2015).

p. 15: On "After My Friend Phyllis Shows Me the *New York Times* Obituary Headline: 'Lou Michaels, All-Purpose Player, Dies at 80, Missed Kicks in '69 Super Bowl,'" the quote is from Wayne Muller's book *A Life of Being, Having, and Doing Enough* (Random House LLC, 2010).

p. 17: On "Wild Rose Steps In at the Circus," in 2011, my good friend Art Goodtimes suggested I needed an alter ego. We had seen Jane Hilberry read a few years before, and both of us had fallen in love with her poetic alter ego, Crazy Jane. What a freeing device it has been! Wild Rose will do everything I am too nervous, too embarrassed, too prude to do.

p. 22: "Inner Mary and Martha" is based on the Gospel story found in Luke 10:38–42.

p. 23: "Going Camping with Audrey Hepburn" quotes are all attributed to Audrey Hepburn.

p. 29: On "Divining," to see the image by Meghan Tutolo, visit https://www.rattle.com/divining-by-rosemerry-trommer/.

p. 36: "Quantum" is based on a line from "Someday I'll Love Ocean Vuong," by Ocean Vuong, from *Night Sky with Exit Wounds* (Copper Canyon Press, 2016).

p. 58: On *"Inc Lak Keig,"* this title comes from the Mayan, "I am the other you."

p. 61: On "It Won't Make the News," to see the image of the painting "Chronicle" by Ruth Bavetta, visit https://www.rattle.com/it-wont-make-the-news-by-rosemerry-trommer/.

p. 80: On "The Precious Matter of Love," the quote from Daniel Ladinsky's version of Hafiz is from "Why Just Ask the Donkey," from *The Gift* (Penguin Books, 1999). Quote reprinted with permission from Daniel Ladinsky.

p. 86: On "Butterfly Effect," in chaos theory, the Butterfly Effect refers to the sensitive dependence on initial conditions, and points to how small causes can have larger effects.

p. 97: On "Picking Up a Hitchhiker in May," the interview with poet/undertaker Thomas Lynch on NPR was on May 6, 2013.

p. 101: "As the Broken Do" was inspired by the line from e.e. cummings, "even if it's sunday may i be wrong," from his poem "may my heart always be open to little," from *E.E. Cummings: Complete Poems 1904–1962* (Liveright Press, 2016).

p. 107: "Autumnal" was inspired by the title "Ask Me," by William Stafford, from his book *The Way It Is: New and Selected Poems* (Graywolf Press, 1999).

ROSEMERRY WAHTOLA TROMMER lives in southwest Colorado and is the author of ten collections of poetry. Her poems have appeared in *O Magazine, Rattle.com, TEDx,* in back alleys, on *A Prairie Home Companion,* and on river rocks she leaves around town. She's taught poetry for Think 360, Craig Hospital, Ah Haa School for the Arts, Weehawken Creative Arts, Camp Coca-Cola, meditation retreats, twelve-step recovery programs, hospice, and many other organizations. She's won the Fischer Prize, *Rattle*'s Ekphrastic Challenge,  the Dwell Press Solstice Prize, the Writer's Studio Literary Contest, and was a finalist for the Colorado Book Award. As Colorado's Western Slope Poet Laureate (2015–2017), she created and curates Heard of Poets, an interactive poetry map. She earned her MA in English Language & Linguistics at UW-Madison. Since 2006, she's written a poem a day. One-word mantra: *Adjust.*

Naked for Tea was a finalist for the 2017 Able Muse Book Award.

Also from Able Muse Press

Jacob M. Appel, *The Cynic in Extremis – Poems*

William Baer, *Times Square and Other Stories;*
New Jersey Noir – A Novel

Lee Harlin Bahan, *A Year of Mourning (Petrarch) – Translation*

Melissa Balmain, *Walking in on People (Able Muse Book Award for Poetry)*

Ben Berman, *Strange Borderlands – Poems;*
Figuring in the Figure – Poems

Lorna Knowles Blake, *Green Hill (Able Muse Book Award for Poetry)*

Michael Cantor, *Life in the Second Circle – Poems*

Catherine Chandler, *Lines of Flight – Poems*

William Conelly, *Uncontested Grounds – Poems*

Maryann Corbett, *Credo for the Checkout Line in Winter – Poems;*
Street View – Poems

John Philip Drury, *Sea Level Rising – Poems*

Rhina P. Espaillat, *And after All – Poems*

Anna M. Evans, *Under Dark Waters: Surviving the* Titanic *– Poems*

D. R. Goodman, *Greed: A Confession – Poems*

Margaret Ann Griffiths, *Grasshopper – The Poetry of M A Griffiths*

Katie Hartsock, *Bed of Impatiens – Poems*

Elise Hempel, *Second Rain – Poems*

Jan D. Hodge, *Taking Shape – carmina figurata;*
The Bard & Scheherazade Keep Company – Poems

Ellen Kaufman, *House Music – Poems*

Carol Light, *Heaven from Steam – Poems*

Kate Light, *Character Shoes – Poems*

April Lindner, *This Bed Our Bodies Shaped – Poems*

Martin McGovern, *Bad Fame – Poems*

Jeredith Merrin, *Cup – Poems*

Richard Moore, *Selected Poems;*
  Selected Essays

Richard Newman, *All the Wasted Beauty of the World – Poems*

Alfred Nicol, *Animal Psalms – Poems*

Frank Osen, *Virtue, Big as Sin (Able Muse Book Award for Poetry)*

Alexander Pepple (Editor), *Able Muse Anthology;*
  Able Muse – a review of poetry, prose & art (semiannual, winter 2010 on)

James Pollock, *Sailing to Babylon – Poems*

Aaron Poochigian, *The Cosmic Purr – Poems;*
  Manhattanite (Able Muse Book Award for Poetry)

Jennifer Reeser, *Indigenous – Poems*

John Ridland, *Sir Gawain and the Green Knight (Anonymous) – Translation*
  Pearl (Anonymous) – Translation

Stephen Scaer, *Pumpkin Chucking – Poems*

Hollis Seamon, *Corporeality – Stories*

Ed Shacklee, *The Blind Loon: A Bestiary*

Carrie Shipers, *Cause for Concern (Able Muse Book Award for Poetry)*

Matthew Buckley Smith, *Dirge for an Imaginary World (Able Muse Book Award for Poetry)*

Barbara Ellen Sorensen, *Compositions of the Dead Playing Flutes – Poems*

Wendy Videlock, *Slingshots and Love Plums – Poems;*
  The Dark Gnu and Other Poems;
  Nevertheless – Poems

Richard Wakefield, *A Vertical Mile – Poems*

Gail White, *Asperity Street – Poems*

Chelsea Woodard, *Vellum – Poems*

www.ablemusepress.com

CPSIA information can be obtained
at www.ICGtesting.com
Printed in the USA
JSHW020521200919
1510JS00002B/3

9 781773 490168